Three Things All People Want

Three Things All People Want

By Patricia Haltley

Three Things All People Want

Copyright © 2014 by Patricia Hatley

Cover by: Keller Graphics

ISBN-13: 978-1500841980

ISBN-10:1500841986

Book Website
www.patriciahatley.com
Email: contact@patriciahatley.com

Give feedback on the book at:
Contact@patriciahatley.com
And
Feedback@patriciahatley.com

Printed in U.S.A

This book is dedicated to my granddaughter
Calleigh Olivia—the child who was not supposed to be.
Your presence reminds us daily that miracles still happen.

"Don't imprison innovation and creativity in leadership tactics
of control, power, and who gets the credit."
#team-orientation #empowerment

TABLE OF CONTENTS

Chapter 1: Three Things All People Want

Three Things all People Want 1

   "Leadership Today Requires Compassion, Empathy, and Integrity"(quote) 2

     Relationships Matter Today—Internally and Externally 3

     Chapter Summary 4

     Works Cited 4

Chapter 2: All People want to be Respected as Individuals!

All People Want to be Respected as Individuals 5

   "We Used to Think of Diversity in Terms of Gender,

     Ethnicity, Age…" (quote) 5

   "Organizations will Pay Millions in Costs Resulting

     from High Turnover…" (quote) 6

Generational Preferences in Diversity Programming

is Critical for Three Reasons 7

   "Empowerment and Collaboration Results in

     a Culture of Innovation and Creativity…" (quote) 8

   "Diversity and Inclusiveness is More

     Than Espoused Programming" (quote) 9

How Can an Organization Create a Culture of

Respect for People as Individuals? 10

Create a Culture in Which Respect for all People is the Rule,

not the Exception 10

Who are "all" People? 11

Develop a Culture of Diversity and Inclusiveness 11

Creating a Sustainable Culture of Diversity and Inclusiveness 12

   "CEO to HR Leader, 'What if we Invest in Training

     and They Leave?" (quote) 13

Hold People Accountable for Behaviors that Support the Culture 13

All Managers are now Leaders as They Have the Responsibility of 14

Chapter Summary 14

Chapter 3: All People Want to Know They are Making a Difference!

All People Want to Know They are Making a Difference!......................... 17

 "A Simple Definition of a Leader Used to Be, 'to Get People
  to Follow…' (quote) 17

Bottom line, the workplace suffers from... 18

 "Younger Generations…Thrive on Instant Feedback…" (quote).............. 18

Today's definition of a leader: 19

Keep these in mind: 20

Remember the "Power of Ask".. 20

Give People Feedback Often and on a Timely Basis—Good and Bad, in a
 Coaching Manner.. 20

Remember: People want to be respected as individuals.......................... 20

Coach and Mentor Instead of Berating or
 Beating People Up When They Make Mistakes..................................... 21

 "When People's Voices are Suppressed…Trust Erodes…" (quote)............. 21

Remember: Your goal as a leader is to help
 your team members succeed 21

Recognize and Celebrate Individual and Team Successes......................... 22

Give Team Members a Voice—Let Them Know
 What They Think is Important... 22

The Power of Ask! Inclusive! Collaborative! Energizing! Inspiring!.......... 22

Remember: It's all about the team, not about you, the boss 23

"Ask" Your Team Members for Thoughts on How
 to Improve Team Performance... 23

"Ask" the Team to Help Develop Goals and Objectives,
 and How to Arrive at Success... 23

"Ask Team Members for Feedback on How you are Doing
 as Their Leader 24

Chapter Summary 25

Chapter 4: All People Need Love:
Love is the Greatest of Human Needs!

All People Need Love: Love is the Greatest of Human Needs! 27

    "Love is the Power of Life. Love Empowers People. A Culture of Love…"

        (quote) 27

    "I Would Contend and Hold True That the Number One Cause of Poor

        Workplace Engagement is Poor Leaders." (quote) 28

    "Compassion, Kindness, and Empathy are the Foundation of a Successful

        Leadership Model Today…" (quote) 29

Love Inspires! Hate Suppresses! 29

A Culture of Love Spawns Innovation and Creativity 30

    "if you do not 'First' Develop a Culture that will Spawn

        and Sustain Empowerment, Your Talented People

        will Become Frustrated and Exit." (quote) 30

Focus on Leadership Quality! Hire and Train for It! 31

Chapter Summary 31

Works Cited... 32

Chapter 5: What Love Looks Like in an Organizational Environment: Love-based Leadership!

What love looks like in an organizational environment:

    Love-based leadership!.. 33

    "When I Refer to 'Leaders," I am also Referring to Managers" (quote)..... 33

    "Love Allows Growth—Individual and Team…" (quote)........................ 34

Focus on Leadership Quality! 35

    "The 'Boss' is De-emphasized, While Focus is Placed

        on 'Team-orientation…" (quote) 35

    "We Need to Move Away from the

        Industrial Age Leadership Styles" (quote) 35

    "Don't be a Seagull Leader…" (quote) 36

Get to Know Your People!.. 36

Schedule One-to-One Meetings.. 36

Have Team Meetings.. 37

Make it a Point to Interact with Your Employees 37

Talk to Your People.. 38

Develop a Culture of Respect for People as Individuals—
Leadership Quality Must be a Priority **38**
Don't Imprison Innovation and Creativity in Leadership Tactics of Control
(quote).. 38
Compare Your Leaders' Results—Good Leaders Versus Bad Leaders **39**
"Help your Team Members Learn to Support Each Other…a Culture
of People Who Are Interdependent on One-another for Success."
(quote).. 39
Develop Rules of Engagement **40**
Give Everyone a Voice **40**
Practice Transparency in Communications **41**
What is Your Intent? **41**
Develop Trust Vertically and Cross-Functionally **42**
"Trust is the One Thing That Changes Everything…" (quote)................. 42
"Love-based Leadership is About Intent…" (quote)................................ 43
Develop Digital Communications Etiquette Same as Verbal **43**
Be Sure Your Digital "Voice" Says What You Mean for it to Say
(quote).. 44
Chapter Summary **45**
Works Cited **46**

**Chapter 6: Knowledge Worker Age: People are
Your Most Valuable Asset**
Knowledge Worker Age: People are your most valuable asset **47**
"We are No Longer in an Industrial Age (quote) 48
You Managed Things; You "Lead" People! **49**
**A Collaborative Culture Results in a Cycle or Spiral
of Continuous Improvement** **50**
"Product Cost Used to Be 80 Percent on Materials…"(quote) 50
Works Cited **51**

Preface

Three Things All People Want

Organizational success today depends on your ability to create an empowered, collaborative culture where your people are fully engaged.

We hear so much about managing Millennials (Gen Ys). One thing we all must remember is that success today is not just about the Millennials. There are many trends and issues driving the need to change cultures and leadership methods if one is to succeed: four generations in the workplace, digital evolution, globalization, leadership style preferences and what is effective has significantly changed, declining birth rates, and the massive population of Boomers exiting the workplace at some 10,000 per day. And, in an age where people-actuation and employee engagement is critical, few organizational and community leaders understand the need for focus on leadership quality. Research has proven that poor leadership quality is the biggest contributor to low employee engagement.

Throughout my career, I have seen incredible talent trapped within cultures where "managers" refused to listen to people. I saw people brutalized by controlling management tactics that in today's world are more and more being seen as emotional abuse. The "managers" in such environments knew it all, or so they thought, and it was "my way or the highway." They yelled, screamed, micromanaged, brow-beat, threatened, and made decisions based on personal needs for power and control.

In such cultures, people were automatons. Energy was minimal. There was no collaboration, empowerment, or learning. There was no innovation and creativity. People were afraid to share their thoughts. They came to work because they needed to earn a living. There was no loyalty. There was constant strife, grievances, back-stabbing, high turn-over rates, and illness. People were oppressed. These were very sick cultures and sick people. The sad thing is that these cultures and leadership tactics are still dominant today—in organizations of all kinds, family structures, and communities.

Organizational leaders recognize the need to create a culture of innovation and creativity, and one in which young people can be effectively integrated. They hire young people and send some of their more tenured team members home. Their young people, ultimately, exit as well leaving the organization to hire and train again. Why? There was no focus on changing the culture to one that will create and sustain innovation and creativity. There was no focus on leadership quality.

An organization is not just machines and buildings and grounds. An organization is filled with people with souls; people who have hopes, dreams, and desires. People should be treated as the unique human beings they are. Treat people with respect and dignity. Strive to tap into the basic needs of your people and you tap into incredible energy, creativity, and innovation that you cannot shut down.

In today's world, driven by a digital revolution that will continue to evolve faster than anyone thought it would, and with the most heterogeneous work force in history, your success depends on your ability to tap into human potential. Your success depends on your ability to "inspire" your people, and maximize their potential. That can occur only by treating people as human beings, not as "things."

Love your people! Love is the greatest of human needs. You can integrate love into every corner of your organization. People will respond and in a very positive way. I heard a CEO who is the fourth generation leader of a family-owned company tell the story of how he kept his company from going under. He said, "I loved my people." As simple as that! "I just put my people first."

All people want to be respected and valued as the unique individuals they are. All people need to know they are making a difference. All people need love; love is the greatest of human needs. Create a culture where these three things are the foundation of everything in the culture and you will tap into incredible energy, employee engagement, innovation, and creativity. All generations and all people respond positively to this.

Love-based leadership nurtures trust. A real culture of empowerment and collaboration evolves in an environment where people trust. It is within such a culture that innovation and creativity is spawned. Learning occurs.

A collaborative environment is a learning environment which creates a spiral of continuous improvement and expansion as new ideas and ways to solve problems evolve. It results in an environment that is self-perpetuating. Put your people first! Everything else will fall into place. Shut down the 'power.' Send the bullies home.

--Patricia Hatley, July 2014

Chapter One

Three Things All People Want

During the course of my research as I completed my graduate leadership program, and continued research for my book *4 Generations @ Work: Leading from Conflict to Collaboration,* (2011), I learned there are three things all people want, regardless of their socio-economic status, ethnic group, position or anything else.

In today's relationship-oriented world, these can be any organization or communities' building blocks to success—Love, respect as individuals, and purpose:

Love is the greatest of human needs.
To be respected as individuals!
To know they are making a difference!

In the Knowledge Worker Age in which we are in now, organizational success depends on your ability to inspire people to the highest level of engagement and maximize people's potential. An empowered, collaborative culture is a must for success—not an exception.

If you create a culture in which these three factors are the end result of programming and accountabilities, you are more likely to tap into individual and team potential.

Authors and leadership gurus Kevin and Jackie Freiberg, in their book *Nuts!* (1996), told the story of Southwest Airlines. Southwest Airlines found incredible success by developing a culture based on "love." "Employees at Southwest are encouraged to be authentic, to be real. They are free to express themselves in real, creative ways and encouraged to influence the uniqueness of Southwest by projecting their own individuality (p. 66)."

Their culture aspires to respect for the individuality, uniqueness, and creativeness of each individual. People are hired to fit this culture. Individuals know they are making a difference to the success of the organization. Individuals know they are valued.

> "Leadership today requires compassion, empathy, and integrity, as well as the courage to do the right thing even when the world says different."
>
> - Patricia Hatley

Important to their success—"love" is the foundation of the organizational culture—from the CEO to front line employees to the way customers are treated.

Southwest's chairman, president, and CEO Herb Kelleher espoused to developing a culture of "leadership in every nook and cranny of your organization." And that's what they did.

Acclaimed author and leadership guru Tom Peters, who wrote the foreword in the Freibergs' book said, "What I discovered is an organization that dares to unleash the imagination and energy of its people…There is a spirit of entrepreneurship—much more than a decentralized organization chart—an attitude that extends to every corner of the company (pg. xv)."

As a result of such a culture, the organization has historically had one of the lowest turnover rates and the most productive work force in their industry. Why?

They put their people first. Employees are respected as individuals, as human beings who have souls and hopes, dreams and desires. People are not mere numbers on an organizational chart. Southwest's leaders saw the value in putting people first over machines and things.

The Freibergs tell us to pay attention to peoples' needs because "…your most valuable resources drive away at the end of every business day, and it is your job to make sure they are eager to return the next morning (p. 37)."

Never has this statement been more true, and will become even more so over the next decade.

RELATIONSHIPS MATTER TODAY—INTERNALLY AND EXTERNALLY.

What's driving it? For some background, read my book *4 Generations @ Work*, content on Knowledge Worker Age, watch my video, and read my blog. We can summarily attribute it to: digital impact, an extremely heterogeneous work force, leadership style tolerance changes, and global economy.

Boomers at some 78 million in the workplace are exiting the workplace at a rate of some 10,000 per day. Gen Ys (or millennials) at near 70 million in the workplace, along with the narrow population of Gen Xers, will be left behind to lead the organizations, communities and non-profit organizations.

The younger generations will not tolerate what is commonly known as "Industrial age" style of leadership which is characterized by top-down, authoritative, fear-based, micro-management, controlling, and tiered to managing "things." And, this style of leadership is not effective anymore. What does get results is a leadership style of empowerment and collaboration.

People are your most valuable asset, not things. And people do not respond well to being treated as "things." They do respond to "empowerment" and being given a voice.

CHAPTER SUMMARY:

Leadership today requires compassion, empathy, and integrity, as well as the courage to do the right thing even when the world says differently.

WORKS CITED:

Hatley, Patricia. (2011) *4 Generations @ Work: Leading from Conflict to Collaboration.*

Freiberg, Kevin and Jackie. (1996) *Nuts: Southwest Airlines' Crazy Recipe for Business and Personal Success.* New York: Broadway Books

Peters, Tom. (1996) Foreword to *Nuts! Southwest Airlines' Crazy Recipe for Business and Personal Success* (pg xv). New York: Broadway Books.

Chapter Two

All People Want to be Respected as Individuals!

All people want to be respected as individuals, not who "you" think they should be. People want to be respected and valued for their individual uniqueness.

We all have a tendency to stereotype people based on pre-conceived ideas of "what" and "who" we think they should be and how they are to act. Most often, we do not realize we are doing it. And, all too often, we are not tolerant of those considered "different" than "me."

This tendency breaks down trust, empowerment, and collaboration; compromises relationships; and, ultimately, results are impacted. We are in an age that values relationships rather than positions and power.

> "We used to think of diversity in terms of gender, ethnicity, age, faith preference, race, etc. Diversity now must include generational preferences and values."
>
> –Patricia Hatley

One of the greatest challenges today and even more so over the next decade is intergenerational collisions due to misunderstandings of generational preferences and values, and stereotyping.

The Boomers say the Gen Ys are lazy, unfocused, dress sloppy, and are unable to solve problems. One of the most often I hear is, "all they want to do is stay on the darned wireless devices." Or, "Gen Ys lack social skills."

On the other hand, Gen Ys have a tendency to immediately cast all Boomers as slow because they generally are not as tech literate as Gen Ys are; Boomers are not as worldly since they did not grow up with access to the world at the digital end of their fingertips; and Boomers are resistant to change.

And, most people say Gen Xers are not team players, they like to work alone, and that they are generally cynical about most things. "They don't play well with others," I hear often.

Research shows that there are some tendencies among the generations to behave as stereotypes portray them.

Yet, research also shows that in the right culture, everyone learns from each other and, as a result, the individual potential of each member is raised to a higher level. Research and my experience also show that in a culture of trust and empowerment, team and organizational results are also improved.

We used to think of diversity in terms of gender, ethnicity, age, faith preference, race, sexual orientation, etc. These all still need to be in the mix. Yet, one thing most organizational and community leaders are leaving out of the mix now is generational preferences and values.

There are four generations in the workplace for the first time in history. Due to the era in which

> "Organizations will pay millions in costs resulting from high turnover, reduced productivity, and legal fees, not to mention payouts for lost legal pursuits."
>
> -Patricia Hatley

each generation grew up in each has tremendous divergent values and preferences, especially the younger generations due to digital impact. This is more so than ever in history due to digital impact on preferences and values.

If leaders do not recognize this and manage it appropriately, conflict occurs. Teams break down! Empowerment cannot be achieved! Collaboration does not occur! Ultimately, the cost of doing business increases exponentially, revenues decline, and shareholder value is impacted.

When I conducted my research for my book, *4 Generations @ Work: Leading from Conflict to Collaboration (2011)*, a survey conducted by the Equal Employment Opportunity Commission (EEOC) showed that over 81 percent of organizational leaders responding to a survey did not consider generational preferences when developing diversity programming.

GENERATIONAL PREFERENCES IN DIVERSITY PROGRAMMING IS CRITICAL FOR THREE REASONS:

1. With Boomers at nearly 78 million in the workplace exiting the workplace at some 10,000 per day over the next decade, Gen Ys and the narrow group of Gen Xers will be left behind to lead the organizations and communities. Succession planning is critical to success, and it is no longer just about the leadership team.

2. By considering generational preferences in diversity integration, an organization also reduces intergenerational conflict which could have a catastrophic impact on morale and productivity, and it has the potential to lead EEOC complaints and lawsuits.

3. "Culture" has never been as important to success as it is now and will become even more so over the next decade. A culture of diversity and inclusiveness, as well as empowerment and collaboration is critical to success. This cannot be accomplished without the right "leaders" in place.

Organizations will pay millions in costs resulting from high turnover, reduced productivity, and legal fees, not to mention payouts for lost legal pursuits.

Another implication is organizational and community reputation which also impact customer loyalty—now more than ever and this trend will increase over the next decade as the Plurals (born between1994-2004) enter the workplace and gain buying power. This group will soon be the fourth generation in the workplace as the Veterans are few in numbers now and quickly exiting.

Younger generations, unlike their parents, are not loyal to brands, but they are to a cause or idea. Brand loyalty is relational and personal—your brand must "speak" to people as individuals and stand for something. Your brand must tell a story? What does your brand mean? What is your story? Does your organizational culture and external image speak to your brand meaning—your brand story?

When speaking to a professional organization membership, a group of university students also joined the meeting to listen and learn. Students were asked to share some of their personal experiences. Unanimously, there was a trend in the comments—a disturbing trend.

"Boomers have a tendency to be intolerant of Gen Ys because they see us as 'different'. As a result we are generally not considered for jobs that often we are more qualified for. All we ask is that you give us a chance."

"My organization hires using a team concept because we found that the Boomer managers and leaders wanted to hire people like themselves. They would not even consider a Gen Y because they see us as being different. And, they do not see the value of creating diversity."

> "...empowerment and collaboration... results in a culture of innovation and creativity, which spawns a cycle of learning and improvement. It is self-perpetuating. This is sustainability in today's world."
> –Patricia Hatley

Divergent thinking is critical to success in today's world. When a culture is one of true diversity and inclusiveness, empowerment and collaboration can be developed. This results in a culture of innovation and creativity, which spawns a cycle of learning and improvement. It is self-perpetuating. This is sustainability in today's world.

> "Diversity and inclusiveness is more than espoused programming and words on a wall. It's a way of life...it has to be embedded into every corner of your organization."
>
> –Patricia Hatley

Different is just different; different is not bad. There are as many cultures in this world as there are people due to how each is raised, ethnic background, education level, experiences, religious beliefs, etc. I am a culture in myself. People should be respected and valued for their uniqueness, and then your organization and community can tap into human potential. It is energizing.

Look at it a different way. The Golden Rule states that we should "treat others as we want them to treat us." Today we need to take this to a higher level and use the "platinum" rule: "Treat others as they want to be treated as they may not wish to be treated as you do." This is true diversity in today's world.

Obviously we need to get to know people, their preferences and values, and keep an open mind and respect for people's uniqueness. People are no longer just numbers on an organizational chart; they are any organization or community's defining competitive differentiator.

And, if you take this thought process a step further, in today's world, organizations need people who are not afraid to move to the opposite end of indifference and intolerance to respect people as individuals. Furthermore, organizations and communities need leaders who have this same mindset.

HOW CAN AN ORGANIZATION CREATE A CULTURE OF RESPECT FOR PEOPLE AS INDIVIDUALS?

Start here:

- Create a culture in which respect for all people is the rule, not the exception.

- Develop a culture of diversity and inclusiveness.

- Have diversity and inclusiveness, as well as intergenerational training for all leaders and managers. (Remember: your manager is a leader in today's Knowledge Worker Age.)

- Provide diversity and inclusiveness, and intergenerational training for all your employees.

- Hold people accountable for supporting behaviors. This must tier all the way to the board of directors and leadership team.

CREATE A CULTURE IN WHICH RESPECT FOR ALL PEOPLE IS THE RULE, NOT THE EXCEPTION

First, organizational leaders decide what the culture is to look like. It should be a culture in which respect for all people is the rule. This starts at the top. The very foundation of this culture should be based on "love," "respect," and "tolerance."

But, leaders alone should not define what the culture, ultimately, will look like. Invite employees from all levels, including front line to be part of this process. Keep in mind that the younger generations thrive on having a voice. All people want a voice in the process. Giving people a voice not only inspires them, but it helps them to learn and grow. It also helps develop trust.

Communicate what you wish to accomplish to all employees and create engagement. Research and my experience show that if team members help develop the process and rules of engagement, they are more likely to own it and bring it to life. All team members feel "included" and "valued" as contributing members of the entire organization.

Some leaders would say, "It takes way too long to get everyone involved." If it is important enough to even think of making the shift to an empowered culture, "make" the time. If you do NOT include your employees in the process, such a culture may never occur. In the least, the time spent to include team members will shorten the time it takes to create such a culture.

WHO ARE "ALL" PEOPLE?

In defining who "all" people are, it should be all stakeholders—employees to colleagues regardless of level within an organization to shareholders to customers to the community at large to vendors. It is everyone your employees and your organization interacts with and impacts.

This should also include all people regardless of their socio-economic status, ethnic background, age, race, rank in your organization or elsewhere, etc.

DEVELOP A CULTURE OF DIVERSITY AND INCLUSIVENESS

Most organizations have diversity and inclusiveness programming. Yet, most diversity and inclusiveness programming doesn't really work.

Just because you "say" you have a culture of "diversity and inclusiveness" does not mean you really have such a culture.

To have a true culture of diversity and inclusiveness, it has to be more than espoused programming and words on a wall. It has to be a way of life for every member of the organization from the board to front-line employees. It must be embedded into every corner of your organization.

I heard this definition of diversity and inclusiveness from a speaker at a diversity conference:

"Diversity is when you are invited to the party. Inclusiveness is when you are asked to dance."—author unknown.

> "Diversity is when you are invited to the party. Inclusiveness is when you are asked to dance."
> –Author unknown.

Diversity is when you are hired or you are asked to serve on a community board or committee. Inclusiveness is when you are given a voice. You are heard and you know you are valued as a team member.

For example, often in community meetings, I have seen women, people of diverse ethnic groups, and young people invited to serve, yet when they try to speak, their ideas are quickly shrugged off as insignificant. They were not given a voice. They were invited to the table to create an image that diversity exists. It was all show and no go. Real diversity and inclusiveness did not exist.

CREATING A SUSTAINABLE CULTURE OF DIVERSITY AND INCLUSIVENESS.

Make it work:

- Develop diversity and inclusiveness programming

- Hire a consultant. Don't try to do it yourself as you are too close to it to look at things objectively. Someone outside your organization can help determine needs that you often cannot see yourself. They also will be objective and will not "cover up" flaws and need areas.

- Include all levels of employees in this process.

- Develop symbolism and celebrations surrounding the meaning of diversity and inclusiveness.

- Have this symbolism and associated messaging visible to all as a constant reminder.

- Develop core values that tier to a culture of respect and diversity and inclusiveness.

- Ensure all employees know what the organization's core values are.

- Make the values a way of life—a living, breathing culture of how the organization does business and how people live.

- Establish accountabilities for people-oriented behaviors, and enforce them— at all levels.

- Provide diversity and inclusiveness training for all, including generational preferences and values.

- Include in diversity and inclusiveness training understanding of generational preferences and values.

- Hire a credible consultant/ trainer, or seek advice. If it's worth doing, it's worth training for it. I saw a quote that says it all: CEO to HR leader, "What if we invest in training and they leave." HR leader to CEO, "What if we don't provide training and they stay?"

> CEO to HR leader, "What if we invest in training and they leave?" HR leader to CEO, "What if we don't provide training and they stay."
>
> –Author unknown.

- Managers are of specific focus as they are leaders to front-line employees.

- Make part of the training to have work group conversations surrounding the meaning of diversity and inclusiveness.

- Create celebrations of diversity to reinforce and help create understanding.

- This could include a specific month of diversity and inclusiveness awareness, including employee and community activities.

- PR and community programming should also focus on respect for individual uniqueness, and diversity and inclusion.

- Celebrate peoples' uniqueness.

- Reinforce why divergent thinking is important to organizational success.

- Invite employees to recommend ways to communicate diversity and inclusiveness, and to create a culture of valuing individual uniqueness. Involve front-line supervisors and employees as well.

HOLD PEOPLE ACCOUNTABLE FOR BEHAVIORS THAT SUPPORT THE CULTURE

To develop a culture of any kind, you need rules of engagement, and then the accountabilities for behaviors that tier to the culture.

There should be no exception regardless of position one may hold within the organization, including board members and the leadership team.

There is no excuse for anyone to be unkind to another, regardless of position or status. This includes leadership styles that tend to be controlling, micro-managing, and bullying in nature. Shut off the power. Send the bullies home.

Start here:

- Develop rules of engagement that tier to respect for all people as individuals, and diversity and inclusiveness.

- Invite team members from all levels to assist with developing the rules.

- Communicate the goal to all employees and get feedback.

- When all team members are aware and included in the process, again, they will be more likely to own it and make it part of their culture.

- Hire for culture and make no exception.

- Provide leadership training for your managers—at all levels.

ALL MANAGERS ARE NOW LEADERS AS THEY HAVE THE RESPONSIBILITY OF:

- Inspiring your front-line employees to the highest level of engagement.

- Maximizing people's potential!

Some of your existing managers will not make it. If after training, mentoring and coaching, their leadership style does not meet the needs of your culture, move them to positions where their talents can be better used, or help them to exit.

CHAPTER SUMMARY:

Remember: Create accountabilities for behaviors that tier to your people-oriented culture and hold everyone accountable. No one should be exempt. Focus on leadership quality. Develop and hire for leadership quality. There's no excuse for anyone to be unkind to another, regardless of position. Shut off the power; send the bullies home. All managers are now leaders as they have the responsibility of inspiring your front-line employees to the highest level of engagement and maximizing people potential.

Chapter Three

All People Want to Know They are Making a Difference!

We all have an inner need for reassurance that we are relevant to those who are part of our lives. We need to know we are a valued member of our team, family, or community. People want to know that what they contribute to the team is helping the team succeed?

More often than not, leaders will berate people for mistakes made, missed quotas, and unmet deadlines. Leaders rarely take time to talk about the things team members do "right"— the successes, however large or small. Nor do they coach and mentor to help maximize people potential.

> "A simple definition of a leader used to be, 'to get people to follow.' Your goal as a leader is to get people to think for themselves—empower them. Now great leaders serve, and develop more leaders..."
>
> —Patricia Hatley

(Note: When I reference "leaders," I am referring to managers as well because managers have to be leaders in today's Knowledge Worker Age.)

If leaders would take the time to honestly praise team members—individually, in front of their peers, and/or as a team—they would make a significant difference to team performance.

Instead, when people only hear the negative, the workplace becomes toxic—an abusive environment. Verbal and emotional abuse!

When someone is constantly verbally abused, they begin to feel inadequate, at times fearful and angry, frustrated, and often suffer from low self-esteem.

In this kind of environment, people are afraid to make decisions on their own—empowerment is non-existent. Collaboration is non-existent. There's no trust, which in itself has to occur before empowerment and collaboration can fully occur.

Bottom line, the workplace suffers from:

1. Poor employee morale;

2. High turnover rates;

3. Poor customer service and quality;

4. Cost of doing business increases;

5. Revenues are lost;

6. Shareholder value declines.

In today's Knowledge Worker Age, success depends on your ability to "inspire" your people to the highest level of performance and maximize individual potential. A verbal and emotionally abusive environment inspires no one.

> "Younger generations... thrive on instant feedback... they grew up in an instant gratification world with everything immediately accessible with a few clicks on a digital device."
>
> –Patricia Hatley

Organizations are filled with human beings with souls who have feelings, hopes, dreams and desires.

One of the most important things a leader can do in today's world is to open doors, pave the way, provide resources, and do everything they can to help others succeed.

I overheard a new team leader say to one of his team members, "What can I do to help you today?" My colleague said, "I have never had a manager ask me that," showing obvious pleasure.

That should be the mindset and mantra of every leader—"My goal as a leader is to help my team members succeed..." Period! Everything else will fall into place.

TODAY'S DEFINITION OF LEADER

Remember: A simple definition of a leader used to be, "to get people to follow." Not anymore! Your goal as a leader is to get people to think for themselves—empower people so they generate new ideas and solve problems quickly close to the customer. Now great leaders serve and develop more leaders. They don't just tell people what to do, how to do it, and when to do it.

You want your people empowered to think and act on their own, to collaborate, create, and make decisions without you. When they work in an environment where they feel threatened and are afraid to make mistakes, empowerment will never occur.

Critical today and even more so over the next decade, is that younger generations will not work in a culture of control, power and micro-management. They will exit very quickly, especially your most talented with interdisciplinary skill sets. They are and will be highly sought after by recruiters.

Keep these in mind:

- Give feedback often, and on a timely basis, good and bad, in a coaching manner.

- Coach and mentor instead of berating or beating people up, when they make mistakes.

- Recognize and celebrate individual and team successes.

- Give team members a voice—let them know what they think is important.

- The power of ask — Inclusive! Collaborative! Energizing! Inspiring!

- "Ask" team members for their thoughts on how to improve team performance.

- "Ask" your team members for feedback on how "you" are doing as a leader.

- Listen to understand, not just respond. The power of Ask!

GIVE FEEDBACK, OFTEN AND ON A TIMELY BASIS--GOOD AND BAD, IN A COACHING MANNER

It is important to give feedback on a timely basis—both good and bad.

Younger generations, especially, thrive on instant feedback.

Younger generations grew up in an instant gratification world with every-thing immediately accessible with a few clicks on a digital device.

Therefore, in a world where success depends on maximizing people's po-tential, it is critical to "constantly" coach and mentor team members.

Ask team members "how" they prefer to get feedback. Some may like face-to-face meetings on a regular basis, while others are fine with telephone calls or less informal digital communications.

Remember: People want to be respected as individuals. Get to know your people. Learn what their preferences and values are. "Ask" them! Give them a voice. Always listen to "understand," not just to respond.

COACH AND MENTOR INSTEAD OF BERATING OR BEATING PEOPLE UP WHEN THEY MAKE MISTAKES

"...when people's voices are suppressed...Trust erodes...people become frustrated and angry. They do not collaborate. They do not innovate and create. People do not learn. Empowerment cannot occur...costs increase and performance suffers."
                                        –Patricia Hatley

Schedule regular one-on-ones with team members to get their thoughts on goals and objectives, learn of obstacles to success so you as their leader can help move barriers to help them achieve their goals, but also to "coach" and "mentor" to close gaps in performance and learning.

Younger generations thrive on learning and love to be coached so they can grow and improve themselves.

These meetings should be two-way in nature—a give and take of sorts—not just you as their leader talking. Commanding, telling, and threatening is not coaching. It is demeaning and destructive to what you are trying to do. These types of behaviors also erode trust.

Coaches and mentors listen more than they talk. They help people learn by talking through situations, events or problems, and weaving the stories of success. But, the mentee helps weave the picture of "best practices," problem solving, and success.

This might be accomplished simply by saying "how would you do it differently next time?" Or, how do you think we should do this? Or, "what would you tell the team so they can learn from this as well. Others may be making the same mistake or having the same challenge.

Remember: Your goal as a leader is to help your team members succeed. Do not browbeat, threaten, or command! Coach and mentor towards maximizing people potential. Ask and listen!

RECOGNIZE AND CELEBRATE INDIVIDUAL AND TEAM SUCCESSES

Praise people. Tell people how much you appreciate their individual contributions. Tell them what they are doing to help the team succeed, and why their actions or successes are important to team success.

Make it a point weekly to recognize individual and team successes, but don't let this impede you from praising individuals at other times. Be sincere! And, if in a team setting when appropriate, invite others to share supporting comments of how the team or individual's actions helped create success.

Celebrate team successes. You don't have to break the bank to create a celebration. It can be as simple as sending an e-card, or hosting a team conference call or web-cast to praise team members. Or, letting the team wear jeans to work after a goal is met.

"Ask" team members how they wish to celebrate successes. "Ask" them what incentives would be meaningful to them.

Let team members develop celebrations, as opposed to you, the leader. You are empowering them, and you are giving them a voice.

GIVE TEAM MEMBERS A VOICE—LET THEM KNOW WHAT THEY THINK IS IMPORTANT

"The Power of 'Ask!'
Inclusive!
Collaborative!
Energizing!
Inspiring!
Priceless!"
   -Patricia Hatley

One of the most powerful things a leader can do to inspire and energize team members is to give them a voice. Everyone has a voice. And, everyone has a need to know that what they think is important to the team's success.

A Gen Y friend who was recently promoted to a leadership role said, "The title is almost embarrassing. It's all about the team and the team's success. It's not about me. I'm just a team member." Well said my friend!

In a Knowledge Worker Age, the "boss" is de-emphasized, and "team-orientation" has become critical. It's all about the team. And, in a culture of empowerment and "team-orientation," all team members have a voice.

Include individuals and the team in decision-making relative to team success, including developing rules of engagement that help determine success.

Listen! Listen! Listen! Successful leaders listen more than they talk. Listen to understand, not just to respond. They learn from their team what the challenges are that impede success. They give team members a voice.

What happens when people's voices are suppressed? Trust erodes. People become frustrated and angry. They do not collaborate. They do not innovate and create. People do not learn. Empowerment cannot occur. Costs increase and performance suffers.

> *Remember:* It's all about the team, not about you, the "boss." The "boss" is de-emphasized, and "team-orientation" rules. People first. Give everyone a voice. Listen to understand, not just to respond. Listen! Ask! Listen!

"Ask" your team members for thoughts on how to improve team performance

In the process of giving people a voice, also "ask" your team members for thoughts on how to improve team performance.

"Ask" the team to help develop goals and objectives, and how to arrive at success.

Don't create the vision, the rules of engagement, and "command" what and how to do it. This does not accomplish anything except make people angry.

This is especially true of younger generations who thrive in an environment of self-expression, autonomy, and collaboration.

Remember: It's about the team, not about you, the "boss." You are just a team member. Ask people to help develop the processes that will achieve results.

"Ask" team members for feedback on how you are doing as their leader

This is a tough one for most leaders, but critical.

Yet, a successful leader will have created an environment of trust where team members feel safe to give honest feedback.

Yes there is the proverbial 360 degree assessment process, but is it really effective? It most cases, I do not think so. For it to be truly effective, I think individuals must WANT to learn and improve themselves through peer or colleague feedback. If it is a forced process, I have not, as of yet, seen it to be effective in developing people.

When a culture of trust exists, and coaching and mentoring is an ongoing process, everyone feels comfortable sharing and giving feedback—to individuals and teams. This is more impactful than 360 degree or other mechanical assessments.

If the leader has the courage and humbleness to ask their direct reports to give feedback on how they are doing as a leader, team trust and cohesiveness is nurtured and elevated.

What can I do better to help the team improve? What and how can I do better to help you? Am I communicating effectively? Do I give you feedback in a manner that helps you and the team? You can develop your own set of questions. "Ask" for feedback individually, or as a team.

When they give you feedback, listen for understanding, not just to respond. Keep an open mind and learn from what is being said.

"Ask" the team and individuals how they would prefer to give you feedback. Some may not feel comfortable giving feedback in a group meeting, but would one-to-one. Vice versa!

When they do give you feedback, take it seriously, make a note of it, and when you have the next conversation, "ask" if you have improved. Get feedback again on where you are in filling in the gaps referenced earlier.

If you have developed a collaborative environment of trust, these conversations should be fun and enlightening.

"Ask" team members for feedback on how you are doing as a leader. Keep an open mind and listen for understanding.

Listen to understand, not just to respond.

CHAPTER SUMMARY

Remember: The Power of "Ask!" *Inspiring! Inclusiveness! Collaborative! Energizing! Priceless*! It demonstrates to people that you value them, that they are important. Their existence matters! It helps people to learn! It helps to develop trust and assists in developing an empowered culture!

Today's leaders "serve," not just get people to "follow." A leader's goal is to empower people to think on their own. A leader seeks to maximize people potential, help teams succeed, and develop more leaders. Give feedback often, on a timely basis, and in a coaching manner. Recognize and celebrate individual and team successes. Give everyone a voice. Ask for feedback on how you as the leader is doing. Listen to understand, not just respond.

Chapter Four

All People Need Love: Love is the greatest of human needs!

Love is the greatest of human needs! This is true regardless of how hard-shelled one may be or the position or status one may have. Love is not bound by where one lives, the ethnic group one belongs to, gender, or age. Love is timeless and border-less.

Love-based leadership has become one of the most important forms of leadership—servant leadership. Successful leaders today "serve" their people to help them succeed.

Today your success depends on inspiring your work force (your people) to the highest level of en-gagement and maximizing people's potential. Most modern day leader-

> Love is the power of life. Love empowers people. A culture of love can breathe new life into any organization.
>
> — Patricia Hatley

ship models evolved from the Industrial Age which is dominantly top-down, authoritative, and fear-based. This style of leadership does not inspire anyone and does not work anymore.

Industrial Age leadership style was designed to manage machines and the people who worked with them. Leaders told people what to do and when to do it.

People had no say (voice) in the process. They were basically automatons. Leaders managed "things." People are not "things" and they do not respond well to being treated as things." Ask yourself how you would feel to be treated like a machine.

Furthermore, Industrial Age leadership methods are also characterized by micro-management, power, control, and fear tactics, all of which tend to suppress people and energy, versus the inspiring nature of servant leadership.

In Gallup's "State of the American Workplace report" released in 2013, some 52% of Americans say they are disengaged in their jobs, and another 18% are actively disengaged.

What is the number one cause of disengagement according to the Gallup study? Poor leaders! (Note: Some people dispute the percentages; however, I would contend and hold true that the number one cause of poor workplace engagement is poor leaders.)

Employee engagement has never been as important as it is now, yet it has become even more challenging to achieve. Younger generations are not generally loyal to the organizations like the Boomers have been; they are loyal to people. Your success is relational!

> I would contend and hold true that the number one cause of poor workplace engagement is poor leaders.
> - Patricia Hatley

It is obvious that organizations must focus on leadership and culture quality.

Managers can make or break your organization as people leave bad managers and bad cultures. People do not leave organizations.

To "inspire" team members, leaders have to aspire to people's inner needs.

Organizations are filled with people who have hopes, dreams and desires. To create a culture of empowerment and collaboration, which is imperative to success today, leaders must seek to maximize people's potential—help them succeed. Fulfilling human needs is necessary to creating commitment, loyalty, and engagement.

Nothing inspires a person more than to know they are genuinely cared about and respected as individuals.

> Compassion, kindness, and empathy are the foundation of a successful leadership model today—not commanding, telling, brow-beating, and threatening. We are in a relationship-driven age and there's nothing about Industrial Age leadership models that speak to developing relationships.
> - Patricia Hatley

Compassion, kindness, and empathy are the foundation of a successful leadership model today—not commanding, telling, brow-beating, and threatening. We are in a relationship-driven age and there's nothing about Industrial Age leadership models that speak to developing relationships.

LOVE INSPIRES! HATE SUPPRESSES!

In a workshop I conducted for a group of law-enforcement leaders, one officer to this topic said, "When your words and actions do not raise people to a higher level, your words and actions tier to hate." He said there is no excuse for treating people disrespectfully. As a leader whose purpose in life is to hold people accountable for obeying the law, he felt "love" works in any environment. Powerful!

In an open-ended question during my research, one question dealt with the kind of leader people wanted to work for. Unanimously, responses were: trustworthy (someone I can trust and someone who trusts me); honest; compassionate; kind; empathic; caring; someone who cares about me as a person, not just a number on an organizational chart; someone who will coach me to help me grow, not just beat me up when I make mistakes, etc.

LOVE SPAWNS INNOVATION AND CREATIVITY

Organizational leaders are beginning to recognize they need teams of empowered people who think for themselves. They are recruiting individuals who possess multidisciplinary skill sets, are technical literate, and who are not afraid to try new things. Their goal is to create an innovative and creative work force.

What most do not realize is that if they do not "first" develop a culture that will spawn and then sustain empowerment, the talented people will become frustrated and exit.

One might liken it to this scenario: You have a vintage automobile that is rusted and long past its prime. You sand it, paint it, and polish it, but the mechanical parts are still the same. It looks very nice on the outside. But, the inside is old and rusty. The core (the culture) is old and worn out. It won't go. It's all show.

The same thing goes for an organization. You can hire the most creative and innovative thinking people. But if the culture has not changed from the machine-aged culture and associated leadership styles, all you have done is put a bandage on your problem. It is not sustainable. You will have invested in new people for nothing.

Start at the top and develop leaders all the way to your front-line employees. Notice I said all the way to your "front-line"

> "...if you do not 'first' develop a culture that will spawn and then sustain empowerment, your talented people will become frustrated and exit."
> –Patricia Hatley

employees. That is critical in today's Knowledge Worker Age as you want to continuously be developing leaders at all levels.

When people are your most valuable asset, you want to maximize people potential. You want your employees, at all levels, to lead themselves and others. You want your employees to think for themselves, to make decisions on their own in taking care of everyday business needs and in taking care of customers.

Furthermore, in helping maximize people potential, you are showing respect for them as individuals. You are helping them fulfill individual needs to succeed.

FOCUS ON LEADERSHIP QUALITY: HIRE AND TRAIN FOR IT

For organizations to succeed in a Knowledge Worker Age, it is imperative to budget for leadership training. Training often is something that is cut from the budget first as it is not seen as a necessity for the organization to succeed. Now, one of the most important things you do as you develop your budget is to include leadership training. Focus on Leadership quality! Hire and train for it.

Love-based leadership inspires trust, which then allows people to freely express themselves. They then feel empowered as they do not fear making decisions on their own. They feel safe to collaborate and create. A continuous cycle of learning and improvement results—a sustainable cycle! The organization and results become self-perpetuating.

CHAPTER SUMMARY

Remember: Love inspires! Hate suppresses! Provide leadership training. The biggest contributor to low engagement is poor leadership quality. When people collaborate and create, a continuous cycle of learning and improvement results—a sustainable cycle evolves. The organization and results is self-perpetuating.

WORKS CITED:

Gallup, Inc. (2013) State of American Workplace: Employee Engagement Insights for U.S. Business Leaders. http://www.gallup.com/strategicconsulting/163007/state-american-workplace.

Chapter Five

What Love Looks Like in an Organizational Environment: Love-based leadership!

When discussing "loved-based" leadership, most often, traditional Industrial Age leaders will roll their eyes and frown admitting total resistance to a softer and gentler style of leadership. Some chuckle and say, "Yeah you get your face slapped and get charged with harassment."

Loved-based leadership is not about a sordid back-room sexual rendezvous. Quite the opposite! It is simply about treating people with respect and dignity, and as individuals—as human beings instead of "things," or machines as Industrial Age leadership models espouse to.

Some also ask, "How do you hold people accountable in such an environment?" People will respond more quickly and accomplish sig-

> Note: When I refer to "leaders," I am also referring to managers as they have to be leaders in a Knowledge Worker Age—they impact engagement of your front-line employees.

> "Love allows growth—individual and team. Love-based leadership advances and empowers others' dreams...enables a true Knowledge Worker Age culture to evolve."
> —Patricia Hatley

nificantly more in an environment where they feel valued, are empowered, and have a voice.

Research and leadership gurus say that in a Knowledge Worker Age culture where people are empowered, organizations can improve productivity by as much as 50%.

I believe that as I have seen it work. But the right culture must exist—a culture that will enable people to feel safe to be themselves. The culture must be a culture of empowerment and collaboration. It must be a culture of trust.

Love-based or servant leadership helps to create an empowered culture more quickly and with sustainable results. It speaks to "others" rather than "self."

Love allows growth—individual and team. Love-based leadership advances and empowers others' dreams. Love-based leadership enables a true Knowledge Worker Age culture to evolve and allows for sustainability.

Some things to remember:

- Hire and train managers for people-oriented leadership skills.

- Get to know your team members.

- Hold people accountable for behaviors that support your culture. This should include zero tolerance for mistreatment of people.

- Develop rules of engagement.

- Give everyone a voice in all processes.

- Practice transparency in communications.

- Develop trust vertically & cross-functionally.

- Develop digital communications etiquette same as verbal.

FOCUS ON LEADERSHIP QUALITY!

> "The 'boss' is de-emphasized, while focus is placed on 'team-orientation.' The role of the 'boss' is now 'how can I help you today.'"
> —Patricia Hatley

Never has leadership quality been as important as it is today and will become even more so over the next decade. Also, managers are now leaders as they have the responsibility of "inspiring" your front-line employees to the highest level of engagement.

If I am redundant in referencing "leadership quality" it's because it is the single most important thing organizations can do to succeed in a Knowledge Worker Age. Leadership quality is our nation's biggest gap to employee engagement and organizational success.

Equally as important is to develop a culture that supports it. One is not sustainable without the other. They are interdependent of one another.

Managers need to "lead," not just manage! Your managers and your culture can make or break your organization. People leave bad managers and cultures; they do not leave organizations. This has never been truer.

Younger generations have little loyalty to organizations, but they are loyal to people they trust. And, they thrive in people-oriented organizations with empowered cultures which allow them the flexibility to think for themselves, and collaborate with others.

Provide leadership training for existing managers. For those who are not coachable, who cannot make the transition from an Industrial Age "manager" to a Knowledge Worker Age "leader," move them to a position to better leverage their talents or help them exit.

Not all leadership training is equal either. Training should focus on "inspired leadership" techniques.

> Remember: We need to move away from the Industrial Age leadership styles to a more empowered, collaborative style of leadership.

"Don't be a seagull leader who flies into the workplace every now and then, craps all over everyone, then flies away leaving behind a mess of broken people. This is not leadership..." –Unknown

I have seen what Industrial Age leadership tactics do to the human spirit—it suppresses individuality and self-expression. It dehumanizes people and restrains people's voices. People do not grow. It is not loved-based leadership? In today's world, I do not call it leadership at all.

In a Knowledge Worker Age culture, the "boss" is de-emphasized, while focus is placed on "team-orientation." The role of the "boss" is now "how can I help you today?" It's all about the people!

Choose your leadership training sources with this in mind.

GET TO KNOW YOUR PEOPLE!

More often than not, within the context of the Industrial Age leadership model, an organization's people are "numbers" on an organizational chart—head count that costs the company. Managers and leaders knew or know little about the "people" behind the numbers. They may know names and what is in the personnel records and nothing more.

Who are the people behind the numbers? What are they interested in when they are not at work? What are they passionate about?

If you can tap into individual passion, you tap into incredible energy. How can you tie the individual's passion to the work environment, not just to create greater engagement for one individual, but to the entire team?

SOME THINGS TO REMEMBER:

Schedule regular one-to-one meetings

Schedule regular one-to-one meetings with your employees to learn what you need to do to help them reach goals, but also to learn about the "real" person.

Have team meetings

If this is not feasible due to the size of the work force, make it a point to have team meetings—even digitally if you must.

> "You cannot create and sustain a Knowledge Worker Age culture without developing new-age leaders— leaders who 'lead' to inspire rather than "manage" people to get them to do what you say through controlling, brow beating, and other fear-based management tactics. This is dehumanizing..."
> —Patricia Hatley

In these meetings, ask each individual to share something about him or herself with the team that no one else knows.

This not only helps you get to know your employees, it also helps your team members get to know each other better. Plus, it shows you are interested in them as individuals.

Have fun while you are together. Don't be an old fuddy duddy. Younger generations are social animals, and love a social environment that is more relaxed and open. Free-spirited!

Play games—playing games also helps your employees get to know each other; and it helps create a spirit of camaraderie as well as a mind-set of "team." It relaxes people's inhibitions and develops trust.

Make it a point to interact with your employees.

Visit the workplace not just to talk about objectives not met, but praise them for successes, get to know your people, and share information that will help them succeed.

I love this quote I heard from a speaker at a conference. "Don't be a seagull leader who flies into the workplace every now and then, craps all over everyone, then flies away leaving behind a mess of broken people…" This is NOT leadership. This is an Industrial Age tactic to attempt to "control" by fear. I've seen it. I've seen how destructive it is to people. Shut it down!

Talk to your people

Get to know them. Ask them about their families. Ask them what they enjoy doing. Ask them for their opinions. The power of "ask."

Ask your employees how "you" can help them succeed at work. "How can I help you...?"

If you do not know answers, admit it. It is powerful for you as a leader to admit you are human. "I do not know the answer to that, but I will find out and get back to you." Make it a point to follow up.

Humbleness is an inspiring strength for a Knowledge Worker Age leader. Don't be afraid to show your weaknesses—it shows you are human just like your employees. It puts you on their level and helps to develop trust.

DEVELOP A CULTURE OF RESPECT FOR PEOPLE AS INDIVIDUALS—LEADERSHIP QUALITY MUST BE A PRIORITY!

Leadership training to develop good leaders is a must when creating a culture of respect. But, it doesn't stop there.

> "Don't imprison innovation and creativity in leadership tactics of control, power, and 'who gets the credit.' Leadership quality and a culture that sustains it must be a key focus. Industrial age leadership is not effective in creating an empowered culture."
>
> —Patricia Hatley

All organizations have cultures within a culture. For example, an organization may have written values that tier to diversity and inclusiveness, and respect for people as individuals, yet the "real" culture and "leadership styles" do not support it.

The dominant modern-day leadership styles were handed down from the Industrial Age where people managed machines—"things." You cannot create and sustain a Knowledge Worker Age culture without developing new-age leaders—leaders who "lead" to inspire rather than "manage" people to get them to do what you say through controlling, brow-beating, fear-based management tactics. This does not inspire and is dehumanizing.

You want empowered people who think for themselves. People will not make decisions on their own if they are afraid if they make mistakes they will be brutalized.

I have seen what this style of leadership does to the human spirit—it breaks people and imprisons "voices," "ideas," and "energy." Under this environment, energy is minimal. You can never maximize people potential because you are not doing anything to help people learn and grow. People have no voice. They are not empowered.

COMPARE YOUR LEADERS' RESULTS— GOOD LEADERS VERSUS BAD LEADERS.

There may be some good leaders who by nature or training are able to create their own inspired culture within the more global fragmented culture.

If you, as their leader, compare the results of the "good leader" work groups with others, you most often will find that these work groups are performing consistently at a higher level. Not only is their performance higher, but you will find customer service is better and pursuit of excellence is higher as there is generally pride in their work.

Cost of doing business is usually less for these work groups due to reduced turnover, grievances, and absences from the workplace. There is generally trust among team members which results in collaboration and a process of continuous improvement—a sustainable cycle.

It goes without saying that if you create a working, sustainable culture of empowerment, performance will increase exponentially.

> "Help your team members learn to support each other instead of walking over a colleague who has fallen—a culture of people who are 'interdependent on one-another for success.'"
>
> –Patricia Hatley

DEVELOP RULES OF ENGAGEMENT

Does your organizational culture have policies that speak to how people are to interact, communicate, and in general treat each other on a day-to-day basis?

In the past, these rules dealt mostly with behaviors that might be considered discriminatory or harassing in nature. These policies, more often than not, evolved due to federal laws regarding such behaviors, not because organizational leaders wanted to make these changes.

An organizational culture that aspires to "love" and respect for all people must also include understandings of intergenerational preferences and values, as well as gender, age, ethnic, etc. It aspires to treating all people as individuals, not what you think they should be based on pre-conceived stereotypes or personal preferences.

This kind of culture is one in which innovation and creativity can thrive and become a way of life because people feel safe to be themselves. People feel safe to make decisions and share without being "brutalized" for making a mistake.

Remember these:

Give everyone a voice in all processes.

- "Ask" for thoughts and "listen" more than you talk. Everyone has thoughts and ideas they are longing to share, but most are afraid to let their "voices" free because of abusive environments which also results in peer ridicule and like behaviors. Put a cap on such behaviors. Zero tolerance!

- Create an environment which allows people to speak freely; to share their ideas. This is where innovation and creativity is birthed. Don't imprison innovation and creativity are leadership tactics of control, power, and "who gets the credit." It's about the team! Team-orientation is critical!

> Don't imprison innovation and creativity in leadership tactics of control, power, and "who gets the credit."
> - Patricia Hatley

- It's all about the "team," not about the boss or who wins, or who is the best.

Practice transparency in communications.

The Industrial Age leadership models emphasize power and control to get people to do and behave as you want them to do, to get people to "follow," not think for themselves!

- Industrial Age leadership uses "power" and "control" tactics which are "fear-based" in nature. Part of this process is holding onto knowledge and information because it is "power" to have the knowledge. It's "controlling" to hang onto the knowledge.

- In a Knowledge Worker age, one does not hold onto information and knowledge, you share it freely with your team so they have all the tools and information they need to succeed.

- It's letting go of the power and control so your team can "go." Literally speaking, this is what it ultimately does. If you micro-manage and attempt to control people—my way or the highway—you are holding them back. You are suppressing their energy and motion. You are also inhibiting personal development.

- There should be no hidden agendas in interactions and communications.

What is your intent?

Is your intent in your actions and words to help your team succeed, or make yourself look better, more powerful?

- Your actions and intent should always be about the "team," never about "self." True Knowledge Worker Age leadership is about "others," it is never about "self."

- When you are "team-oriented" you are always consciously thinking about how you can help individuals and your team succeed. You are always:

   1. Opening doors

   2. Paving the way

   3. Knocking down barriers

   4. Sharing knowledge and resources for the good of the team

   5. Coaching and mentoring to help team members maximize their potential

6. Helping team members learn to support each other instead of walking over a colleague who has fallen—a culture of people who are equally "interdependent on one-another for success."

One might think about the military mantra of "no man left behind." Help each other succeed and the team succeeds.

7. You can be tough as a leader and still treat people with respect. When trust exists, this is easier to accomplish.

DEVELOP TRUST VERTICALLY & CROSS-FUNCTIONALLY

Stephen Covey (2008), in his book The Speed of Trust, says that "Trust is the one thing that changes everything….Trust produces speed."

Why? Because when a group of people—within any organization, family, community, etc.—trust each other, things get done very quickly because people share and collaborate freely. A culture of true empowerment can be arrived at.

Trust also improves individual self-esteem and helps maximize individual and team performance. "High trust is like the leaven in bread, which lifts everything around it (pg. 19)," Covey said.

In the absence of trust, there's a culture of suspicion where everything suffers: employee self-esteem, collaboration, innovation, communications, execution, and relationships with all stakeholders. Ultimately, the organization's results decline which impacts shareholder value.

> "Trust is the one thing that changes everything...High trust is like the leaven in bread, which lifts everything around it."
>
> –Stephen R. Covey

Developing a culture of trust is critical to creating a people-oriented culture which spawns empowerment and collaboration. In such an environment, your people will feel good about being there. It's no longer just a job; it's a good "part of my life." Love based leadership and a culture of love is critical to developing trust.

Equally as important to an empowered culture, is cross-functional collaboration.

Some leaders hang onto the mindset of "team" as being "just my direct reports." As a result, everyone outside their immediate "team" is considered the "enemy." Cross-functional collaboration does not occur. A hostile environment exists. People outside the "team" do not want to interact with the "hostile" team because there is always conflict. And, there's no trust.

If your people are not collaborating cross-functionally—on all fronts—you have silos that inhibit your organization from developing a collaborative culture. Such a culture is detrimental to your organization's success.

> Remember: Love-based leadership is about "intent" in your actions and words. Your "intent" should never be about self; it is always about others. Develop a culture where everyone is equally interdependent on one another for success.
>
> Create an organization-wide, one-team mindset.

Create a culture where all people are equally interdependent on one another for success—everywhere. Develop an organization-wide, one-team mindset.

DEVELOP DIGITAL COMMUNICATIONS ETIQUETTE SAME AS VERBAL.

We are in the midst of a digital revolution in which most often we are communicating via a digital device across a digital platform instead of face-to-face or even voice-to-voice. This will increase in intensity over the next decade rather than declining.

We do not have the benefit of observing body language which is most often more powerful than the spoken word. Nor do we have the benefit of hearing changes in voice inflection due to emotions. We have "silent" words tossed at one another in a host of venues.

Digital communications is the new "voice." But, your voice is loud. With a few clicks of keys on a keyboard, you can send a message through the cyber world that reaches millions of people around the world.

The CEO of a Fortune 500 company can operate his or her business within the confines of the home without ever leaving it. One can lead teams literally around the world without ever seeing one's team members, or ever "speaking" to them one-to-one other than digitally. It's called borderless leadership.

> Often, in an attempt to get things off our desks, we do not think about the "tone" of our "voice."
> - Patricia Hatley

Most often, we forget there is a human being on the other end of the keyboard. We are all doing more with less, and multi-tasking ruthlessly, or as someone said, we are "toggling" from device to device or platform to platform, always with keys. We fire off one email, text message, instant message or social media post after another as we attempt to manage the deluge of varied communications that we must manage or choose to participate in.

I saw a Facebook post that dealt with new-age parenting. It read, "Don't you TYPE at me in that tone of voice!" As humorous as it sounds, it is true that everyone is dealing with digital impact.

Be sure your digital "voice" says what you mean for it to say. Often, in an attempt to get things off our desks, we do not think about the "tone" of our "voice."

The result is a thread of seemingly harassing, abusive, dehumanizing "voices" that have the same effect as voice commands and fear-based methods that are common in Industrial Age leadership models.

> Be sure your digital "voice" says what you mean for it to say. Often, in an attempt to get things off our desks, we do not think about the "tone" of our "voice."
> - Patricia Hatley

Create rules of digital engagement just like you would for face-to-face interactions.

Hold people accountable for behaviors that support these rules of engagement.

But, start by communicating and coaching people to think about their digital communications as their "voices."

And, for heavenly days, every once in a while, take the time to just pick up the phone and call, especially if it means enhancing relationships. Encourage your people to do the same.

In this same thought process, remember to consider individual communications "preferences" when communicating, whether it is internally to colleagues, to customers, to vendors, or to stakeholders. For example, some may prefer and trust a voice call as opposed to an email or text. And, some may prefer and trust only a face-to-face conversation, especially early in the relationship-development process.

Remember, success in today's world is about relationships and trust, but this is difficult to achieve via digital communications if you do not have an awareness and understanding of "how" to communicate for success digitally. It can be a killer to your culture, collaboration and empowerment, customer-service, and, ultimately, to organizational success!

Remember: There's a human being with feelings on the other end of the digital network and platform you are communicating across.

Before you press send, ask yourself if your "voice" is saying what you wish it to say.

Does your voice inspire or does it chop someone off at the knees? Does your voice help develop relationships or does it compromise relationships?

Sometimes, just pick up the phone and call if it helps to develop and improve relationships.

Consider individual communications preferences as you communicate. Some may prefer and trust a voice call, or even a face-to-face conversation, especially early in the relationship-development process.

CHAPTER SUMMARY

Focus on leadership quality. Hire and train managers for people-oriented leadership skills—inspired leadership. Get to know your people. Develop a culture of respect for people as individuals. Develop rules of engagement and accountabilities to support and sustain your culture. Give everyone a voice. Develop a culture of trust; love-based leadership and styles are critical to a culture of trust. Develop digital communications etiquette same as verbal communications etiquette.

WORKS CITED:

Covey, Stephen M.R. (2008) *The Speed of Trust: The one Thing that Changes Everything.* New York: Free Press

Chapter Six

Knowledge Worker Age:
People are Your Most Valuable Asset

We are no longer in an Industrial Age which was characterized by machines. We are in an age characterized by ideas and thoughts—Knowledge Worker Age as it is most commonly known.

No longer are machines and things an organization's most valuable asset—people are. An organization's human capital or intellectual capital is its most valuable asset.

When your people are your most valuable asset, it goes without saying that your success depends on your ability to maximize human potential. I don't like to call people "capital" as it sounds cold and has undertones of "people" as "things" like machines.

People are not machines or things. People do not respond well to being treated like machines either. An organization is filled with human beings with

> "We are no longer in an Industrial Age which was characterized by machines. We are in an age characterized by ideas and thoughts—Knowledge Worker Age...People, not machines, are your most valuable asset...You manage 'things.' You 'lead' people."
>
> –Patricia Hatley

souls—people who all, as divergent as they may be, have hopes, dreams and desires. Organizational leaders tend to forget that and think of their people as numbers on an organizational chart, or mere overhead.

Instead, let's say that your success depends on your ability to maximize people's potential.

Your success in a Knowledge Work-Age depends on your ability to inspire your people to the highest level of engagement and performance. This age values "intellectual capital."

This age values "relationships." Your success depends on your ability to develop relationships—with your employees, customers, vendors, shareholders, communities, etc. It's a world of relationships and success depends on your ability to develop trust, which in turn, inspires people to want to work for you and with you, fight for you, do business with you, invest in you, and so on and so on.

The days when buildings, machines, and "things" are your most valuable assets are gone—forever. We will never go back to that environment. People are your most valuable asset, not material possessions. People matter! Relationships matter!

Yet, most modern-day leadership models and thinking evolved from the Industrial Age where people managed "things" and "machines." Managers kept machines going, and "told" people what to do and they did it. Then they punched the clock to go home. They came back the next day to do it all over again. They did not question the "whats" and "hows" of the organization. Nor did they share their thoughts and ideas on how to improve things. They were not allowed to think and share their thoughts.

That was okay in a dominant machine-driven industrial era. In today's service-intensive, fast-moving global economy, that no longer works. We need to be able to make decisions fast in a highly flexible and fast-moving environment. You cannot do that in an Industrial Age environment of "do as I say or the highway" culture.

Also, people's leadership style preferences have changed. People will no longer tolerate a top-down, authoritative, fear-based style of leadership, especially the younger generations.

YOU "MANAGE" THINGS; YOU "LEAD" PEOPLE!

Acclaimed leadership author Stephen R. Covey wrote, "If I could have people understand one key paradigm of the Knowledge Worker Age, it would be that you manage 'things,' but you lead 'people.' That is how we empower them."

In a Knowledge Worker Age, success literally begins by empowering others. Organizational cultures must evolve to become one where people are interdependent on one another for success. Everyone within the organization is accountable to everyone else.

You could look at it like this: In the Industrial Age, the "leaders" developed the vision and then told the workers what to do, how to do it, and when to do it. Workers did not "think" for themselves; they had no voice.

In the Knowledge Worker Age, the vision may be developed by the leadership team, but the employee body helps develop how to make the vision come to life. Or, the vision evolves from the front-line up to the leadership team in collaborative think processes. Everyone is empowered to think and act. Everyone has a voice.

The organizational world has moved from a "boss-centered" culture to a "team-oriented" culture. It's not all about the "boss" or "leaders," it's about the entire "team."

Even the term "knowledge" is defined differently in a Knowledge Worker Age. Knowledge is no longer about what it is or what it can do, nor is it about developing things and storing it. It is about collaborative thinking. Knowledge, solutions, ideas, innovative and creative thinking evolve from collaboration. It's about creating and sharing knowledge.

A collaborative culture results in a cycle or spiral of continuous process improvement, as well as the evolution of new products, services, and customer solutions. It also unleashes incredible energy, talent, resourcefulness, and new ideas. It's incredible what an inspired, empowered group of people can do.

The dominant thought process is that a real Knowledge Worker Age culture can outperform an Industrial Age culture fifty times. This is because "everyone" is thinking and acting on their own instead of waiting to be told what to do, how to do it, and when to do it. It is also because people are "inspired" instead of "suppressed." It's about "inspiring" people, not "motivating" people.

> "Product cost used to be 80 percent on materials and 20 percent on knowledge; now it's split 70/30 the other way. People are your most important asset."

Organizations are also leveraging technology, which helps improve efficiencies and production. Product cost used to be 80 percent on materials and 20 percent on knowledge; now it's split 70/30 the other way. People are your most valuable asset; not "things."

Obviously, there must be a shift in the organizational world from the Industrial Age leadership styles to one that is more of a servant leadership-oriented style.

Furthermore, your front-line "managers" must now be "leaders" as they are responsible for inspiring your employees who interact directly with and take care of your customers every day. In today's world, your front-line managers can make or break your organization.

But, change must start at the top with a belief and understanding that change must occur and occur now. Then leaders must seek the external help to design the culture that works, then engage all employees in the process of developing the culture.

The old adage "change starts with me" is true, more so now than ever. Change must start with me, the CEO or board of directors' chair, and then include the top-ranking leaders in the vision. After that, "change starts with me," which is every employee in your organization.

But most importantly, change begins by recognizing that your success begins and ends with your people. Your people are your most important asset. Treat them as such. Then create a culture and leadership focus that aspires to people and sustains this belief.

WORKS CITED:

Hatley, Patricia. (2011) *4 Generations @ Work: Leading from Conflict to Collaboration.*

Covey, Stephen R http://sourcesofinsight.com/lessons-learned-from-stephen-covey.

www.ingramcontent.com/pod-product-compliance
Lightning Source LLC
Chambersburg PA
CBHW051238170526
45165CB00004B/1482